MeBook

TOWARD A MEANINGFUL MOOD

Turning Your Dark Moments into Light

Exclusive Gift to Reader

To put you in a GREAT mood, here is an absolutely FREE yet priceless offer exclusive to you, our cherished *MeBook* reader.

How to Have Your Prayers Heard is a magnificently designed, user-friendly handbook that makes prayer accessible while bringing it alive.

Prayer is called "service of the heart." This gift to you from us is our heart connecting with yours.

Simply click here to access it.

~~~

If the URL above is not visible, please visit
www.meaningfullife.com/howtopray

Praise for the Meaningful Life Center

"I am so grateful for the Meaningful Life Center. I am feeling a shift that I have really needed for a long time. You have woken me up to the truth of my own self, giving me the strength to finally heal from a personal trauma I was internally holding onto for many years. I grow as a person every time I visit the site and drink of the waters of wisdom."
- Ikira Donovan, UK

"Thank you for extending an anchor of sanity into this ocean of extreme polarity".
- Patricia Polle, USA

"The Meaningful Life Center is a source of wisdom, comfort and understanding. The variety of topics discussed has made me aware of a very wonderful broadening of my personal life mission. Thank you for touching my creative, searching soul."
- Anne Holstein, Australia

"Your work is truly a life changing inspiration to me. As I am busy as an orthopedic surgeon and don't often have time to read, but I make time for MLC and gain so much from the infusion of spirituality, it provides a tremendous richness to my life."
- Richard Berns, USA

Table of Contents

Preface — Electric Books

What Is a *MeBook* and Why Should You Read One?

This is the book of the chronicles of the person . . .
—Genesis 5:1

I must say I find television very educational.
The minute somebody turns it on, I go to the library and
read a good book.
—Groucho Marx

The Meaningful Life Center (MLC), named for the iconic, best-selling book, *Toward a Meaningful Life*, builds bridges between eternal ideas and contemporary audiences. Using our time-tested methods and proven formulas, we endeavor to articulate heavenly wisdom in relatable language so that you may live a more meaningful life.

The Meaningful Life Center provides indispensable life tools to maximize your highest potential, overcome personal barriers, and transcend life's obstacles. MLC is known for its content, articles, essays, videos, classes, and books that provide deep and meaningful perspectives on life in general, and your life in particular.

With the burgeoning of electric content consumption — think Netflix, Amazon Prime, various streaming devices, Amazon Kindle, and news and books on your smartphone—we at the MLC office asked ourselves a question: Why not create an eBook library of profound content, marrying what we do best (meaningful and relevant life skills) with a practical and growing outlet in eBooks?

You hold in your hand—perhaps in smartphone or tablet form—the answer to that question: the pilot MeBook of what we hope to be an everlasting series of eBooks conveying essential Meaningful Life Center content to the online consumer and tech generation—the eGeneration if you will.

We have called this endeavor: *MeBook*—an eBook infused with the "me" of meaning, and the "me" of a personal and relevant message.

If you like Simon Jacobson's best-selling books <u>Toward a Meaningful Life</u>, <u>60 Days</u>, and *The Spiritual Guide to Counting the Omer*, you'll love the MeBook series. MeBooks are eBooks that address topics and issues close to a person's heart, providing you with indispensable tools and exercises to make drastic improvements in your life—mentally, emotionally, and spiritually. From love and relationships, to career and anxiety, this ever-growing library will help you grow as a person. Based on Kabbalah, this MeBook uses 4,000 years of knowledge, humor, and direct communication to help you change your life quickly.

The MeBooks project endeavors to provide a fresh, unique, and meaningful perspective on the subject at hand. By no means should MeBooks be considered comprehensive or exhaustive overviews of the subjects discussed in them. MeBooks aim to add a new layer of insight, based on thousands of years of meaningful wisdom, not to replace the existing contemporary literature on any particular topic.

Every MeBook promises to offer timeless ideas in timely language. In addition to riveting and relevant content, in every MeBook you will find:

- Quotes on the topic, from both ancient wellsprings and current sources;
- Footnotes from whence our ideas sprang;
- Checklists of what you, the reader, have learned and how to apply it;
- Links to relevant material;
- MeXercises: fun and user-friendly meaningful exercises to help implement what you have learned;
- MeDitations: meaningful meditations to lend tranquility and mindfulness;
- As well as a cornucopia of insights, anecdotes, and tidbits for your betterment and pleasure.

In our first MeBook (Meaningful + eBook = MeBook), we chose to address the topic of moods in general, dealing specifically with bad moods and transforming them into ones that are good. Playing off the title of the best-selling book, *Toward a Meaningful Life,* we have (we think) aptly titled this pilot MeBook, *Toward a Meaningful Mood.*

Why Did We Choose Moods?

Everyone has moods: good moods, bad moods, high and lows. A big part of life is balancing our moods— appreciating the bright moments and dealing with the duller and darker ones.

Piloting the MeBook revolution by analyzing and addressing bad moods, we hope to bring real, meaningful solutions to a very personal and pertinent issue. Our goal is for you, the reader, to supplement your arsenal so that next time you are faced with a dark disposition you will be armed with illuminating skills to understand and transform it.

This one MeBook will, with heaven's help, be the first of many, bringing the Meaningful Life way to the technological wonders at your fingertips.

Thank you for being an integral part of this journey. We hope that these MeBooks will bring more meaning into your personal life and, by extension, more meaning into the world at large.

Together, this hope will certainly become reality.

Part I — What is a mood?

Do aspects of your relationships, job, or life bring out the bad mood in you?

Anxiety in a person's heart: cast it down, and a good word will make it cheerful.
—Proverbs 12:25

Human behavior flows from three main sources: desire, emotion, and knowledge.
—Plato

After reading this MeBook, there is a very good chance that you, dear reader, will find yourself to be in a good mood. With offerings like "The Tripod of Your Life," fill-in charts, and takeaway practical MeXercises, *Toward a Meaningful Mood* will cast moods in a whole new light, while empowering you to use them for personal growth.

Before we address why we have moods and how to use them meaningfully, we must first ask a fundamental question: What exactly is a mood?

The dictionary defines a mood as "a state or quality of feeling at a particular time." A mood, broadly put, is how you feel at a given time. Receiving a good piece of news usually makes you feel good, resulting in a good mood, while a bad piece of news usually makes you feel bad and results in a bad mood.

The science on moods is in flux. Much research has been done on what makes people happy or sad.[1] Is a good or

---

[1] See, as one example,

bad mood the result of chemical balance or imbalance?[2] Is it perhaps an emotional thing, or maybe intellectual, neurological, ideological, experiential, environmental, or philosophical?[3]

The literature on feelings and moods is vast and growing still more vast. As mentioned in the preface, the MeBook aims to contribute a new, meaningful perspective on moods, one that hopefully does not subtract from but adds to the substantial literature, studies, and research being done across the manifold sciences and various other disciplines.

For the sake of our objectives—turning bad moods into good, and transforming dark moments into light—we may broadly define a mood as the general description of how you feel at a given moment: when you feel up, you are in a good mood, and when you feel down, you are in a bad mood.

The Bad Mood: Its Cause(s)

If a mood refers to the state or quality of a human's feelings, then so long as a human is feeling, a human is having a mood. This means that the levels of mood, their seriousness or severity, their causes or effects, vary as much as the human condition. We therefore must

---

http://www.pnas.org/content/107/38/16489.full; https://learning.blogs.nytimes.com/2010/10/07/can-money-buy-you-happiness/?_r=0.

[2] See *Proust Was a Neuroscientist* and *How We Decide* by Jonah Lehrer.

[3] See *The Relationship Handbook*, Chapters 4–5, by George Pransky.

differentiate between moods, the seriousness of their causes, and their varying degrees of impact on our lives.

Bad moods may be caused by almost anything. A bad mood may be caused by the frustration of trying to find love, or by a fight with a loved one. It may have been caused by the despair of losing a job, or by a miserable day at work. Carpooling in bumper-to-bumper traffic may ignite a bad mood. Trying to procure a mortgage, or struggling to cover it, may bring about a bad mood. Feeling empty or feeling overwhelmed, working too hard or working too little, aimlessness, meaninglessness, hopelessness, discord, disillusion... Any and all of these at any particular time may cause a bad mood.

The magnitude of life's expectations, the emptiness of its voids, or a splitting headache may cause a bad mood. Causes are everywhere and are easily intensified.

There are bad moods that have relatively minor causes—like stubbing your toe, or traffic—and there are bad moods that are caused by serious problems, like health issues, financial troubles, or existential crises.

A bad mood that is caused by something ephemeral and transient—say a flat tire—is different than a bad mood caused by something more serious, like the loss of a job or a complicated relationship. A bad mood caused by a stubbed toe will pass rather quickly, and harping on it will only exasperate it. But to ignore a bad mood caused by a severe root cause will not make that bad mood go away, and it certainly will not solve the root problem.

Here is a MeQuestionnaire to help you define your bad mood so that you may then, later in this book, redefine it.

The Bad Mood Questionnaire

Question: What caused your bad mood? Check only those that apply.
Answer:

Work __	Spouse __
Money __	Money __
Purposelessness __	Illness __
Presumed Failure __	Broken friendships __
Other __	

Question: How does your bad mood make you feel?
Answer: _____

Question: How long did your bad mood last?
Answer: _____

Question: Does your bad mood change your core personality, causing you to do things you normally would not? If yes, in what way?
Answer: _____

Question: How does your bad mood differ from a good mood?
Answer: _____

Question: Are you wallowing in your bad mood, or embracing a proactive solution?
Answer: _____

The Bad Mood: Its Misery

In the miserable throes of your bad mood, you probably wouldn't care about its cause or what exacerbated it. In the heat, or melancholy, of a bad mood, you often want simply to indulge yourself in negativity and hope the mood will pass.

Yet a bad mood affects everything in its path. It brings you down and darkens your aspirations. It causes you to lash out at the ones you love, making them, and yourself, miserable.

The question is: Do you wish to remain miserable? The answer: Certainly not! It is time to reject misery and begin living a life of good moods, a chain connected by links of meaningful moments.

> **MeDitation:** To begin turning a bad mood into a good one, breathe in a substantial inhalation and gather with it all the misery, uncaring disinterest, apathy, and any other negative feeling associated with—and caused by—your bad mood. Breathe it in very deeply and gather it in very close. Then breathe out forcefully, loudly, exhaling with conviction, projecting every negativity outward and expelling it from your being. Visualize the swirling breeze that will carry it far away from you over the horizon. Breathe out, feel the release, and smile. As we shall see a little later on, the act of smiling in and of itself is a great way to begin remedying and overcoming a bad mood.

Part II — Having Moods vs. Being MOODY

What are moods and why do I have them?

And it shall come to pass on that day that there shall be no light, only disappearing light and thick darkness.
—Zechariah 14:6

The word "happy" would lose its meaning if it were not balanced by sadness.
—Carl Jung

Why Do I Have Moods?

Every human being, yourself included, has a core—an essence—that is his or her deepest self. It is the innermost flicker of your being, the engine that drives you, the awe and wonder of life you sometimes feel but can never really articulate. Some call it a spark, some a spirit, some the inner child, or an inner music. Some don't call it anything at all.

Let's refer to it here as the soul. Your soul is who you are when you are by yourself, when you are in touch with your essence, when everything else is stripped away.

Your soul has much to say. One of the ways your soul speaks is through moods: artists through their paintings, musicians through their music, and good friends through their love. When you have something to say, you open your mouth to speak. When your soul has something to

15

say, one of its methods is communicating through your moods. Put another way, your soul is multilingual; and one of its languages is the language of moods.

When you are physically hungry and your stomach begins to grumble, it is your body telling you to eat. When you are *emotionally* parched or spiritually hungry, your mood begins to grumble. This is your soul telling you that it is hungry for something, that it is missing an essential ingredient or nutrient.

The same is true in the positive sense: when you eat something delicious, your body feels sated and satisfied. When you experience something beautiful, your soul is joyous and you are in a good mood.

In sum, then, why do you have moods? So that your soul, the spiritual spark that resides in your core being, can communicate with you and keep you in touch with how you feel.

> **MeDitation:** Take pen and paper in hand and list (at least) five good things that have resulted from a bad mood you have had. (Examples: a bad mood could make you realize that you are in an unhealthy relationship or a suffocating job; a bad mood could be a catalyst for change; a bad mood could remind you that you have dreams that you need to fulfill.)

Where Do My Moods Come From?

Everything you encounter, from the color of the sky to the shape of a human face to the length of your bed, is registered in your brain. That raw data is then processed by your mind, which in turn elicits an emotional reaction. Your mood is created by way of your subjective emotional reaction to the objective data you interact with. It comes from your soul reacting to how you live, what you are doing, the type of relationship you are in, and other similar core issues.

When your soul experiences inconsistencies, negativity, or conflict, a bad mood results. When your soul experiences positivity and harmony, a good mood prevails.

Moods also come from the data and emotion you are—or think you are—exposed to.

What Would I Look Like Without Moods?

What would a human body look like with a compromised or nonfunctioning nervous system? Simply said, it would not look good. In fact, it would be a life-threatening condition.

Similarly, your soul would be mute without moods, and without moods you would be unable to hear your deepest self. Even worse, without moods, your *soul's* nervous system would be compromised. You would never know if something were wrong or, for that matter, if something were right.

Knowing why you have moods, where they come from, and what you would be like without them, is imperative to overcoming bad moods and changing them into good.

Humans vs. Computers

The great mystics refer to human begins as "communicators," "those who speak," or "relaters," whose greatest and most essentially human asset is the ability to connect and communicate with other human beings in a personal and relatable way. Furthermore, we are taught that when we breathe, we connect with the oxygen around us. When we eat, we connect with and relate to the mineral, vegetable, or animal we are eating. This holds true with every interaction we have: we relate to other human beings and we are, in turn, related to each other.

Moods are paramount in this connective process, enabling you to relate to and communicate with your self and with the world around you. Moods allow you empathize, to feel, to know, and to discern when something is good and, conversely, when something is not at its best.

Thanks in large part to moods, you have the ability to take something outside of yourself—a tree, a car, an animal, heaven, earth, a person, anything—and connect with it. Computers cannot connect to anything the way you can. Your moods—the way you internalize scenarios and make them personal—are your uniqueness.

Computers, while they are great data processors, do not have moods. Computers do not feel good or bad. Computers do not jump and down with excitement when they receive new software, nor do they pout when a virus infects them. Though computers can help you relate and connect emotionally, they themselves cannot connect emotionally with anything.

Your moods, then, are essential for relating to and connecting with the world around—and within—you.

Objective Data and Subjective Moods

MeXercise: Identify one truth you know for sure to be an objective fact. For example: Water is wet, or ice cream is cold. Now, isolate one positive emotional reaction you have had to that objective fact: The pleasure you felt when you jumped into that wet pool, or the childish glee you felt when you licked that double-fudge ice cream cone. Then, isolate one negative reaction you had to the same objective fact: the frustration you felt when you got stuck in that terrible rainstorm and ruined your shoes; the disappointment you felt when you dropped that ice cream unto the sidewalk; or, perhaps, the guilt you felt after eating the whole thing despite your commitment to your new diet.

This MeXercise highlights the differences between objective data—wet water and cold ice cream, which are devoid of moods and any emotional reaction—and the subjective reactions we have to them, and the resulting subjective moods.

An objective fact is equally true for every single person on planet earth. Water is wet whether you are old or young, male or female, living in New Mexico or New Zealand; ice cream is cold if you live in an igloo in Antarctica or a mud hut in the Sahara. But no two individuals relate to that wet water in quite the same way. Your mood depends on how you react to and interact with the objective data.

Why does this matter? How will this help you transform and transcend your bad mood?

Let's look at an example. Johan receives a letter delivered to him by his postman, Mario. After reading in the letter that the publisher rejected his manuscript,

Johan breaks down in tears. Mario, the sneaky postman that he is, was reading the same letter over Johan's shoulder. While Johan was obviously saddened by the letter, Mario was rather unmoved.

Why is this so: Were not Johan and Mario digesting the same objective data? Yes. However, their personal and emotional reactions to that data were very different.

This is because a bad mood is a *subjective* reaction to a set of objective circumstances. This also means that if one were to alter the set of objective circumstances, one would also alter the subjective response. Furthermore, the fact that Mario is not emotionally affected by the destiny of Johan's manuscript means that on some level, Johan could also transcend his emotional response to the objective data and subsequent subjective bad mood, by seeing the objective data in a different light.

If Moods Are Good, Why Are They Bad?

In and of themselves, moods are not negative; in fact, they are the opposite of bad. What they really are is a reflection of the complex, multifaceted person that you are. The question then isn't, "Why do I have these moods?" Rather, the questions are:
1) How can I turn any negative feelings and bad moods into positive ones and good ones? 2) How can I ensure that my moods, which are part and parcel of my humanity, are positive (that is: *good!*)? 3) What can I do to control my moods and not be controlled by them?

Moods are essentially a part of who you are. Moods are the way your soul communicates. The challenge then becomes getting to know your soul, so that you and your soul can communicate on a high and illuminated level. You don't want to combat your moods; you want to understand and elevate them, and turn the bad into good. Moods can be your greatest ally in navigating life.

MeDitation—Echocardiogram: Draw a straight, flat, horizontal line across a piece of paper. On another paper, or below that line on the same paper, draw another horizontal line—only this one should not be flat or straight; it should have peaks and valleys, up and downs, similar to a stock market graph.

Comparing the two lines, ask yourself this: Which one of these lines would I prefer to see if this were a reading of my heart: the flat line or the pulsing line? Obviously, there is only one rational answer, and that of course is the pulsing line. Why is this the only healthy answer? Because a flat line means a lifeless heart, while a reading that has fluctuations, ups and downs, means that there is a beating, living heart.

The same is true with your disposition: Experiencing no moods, or only one continuous flat mood, is the opposite of living. Like the beating of your heart, the ups and down of moods mean that you are alive.

MeXercise: To bring this point home, on another piece of paper, make a list of all the moods you had today: the good, the bad, the frustrating, and the beautiful. Then attach its perceived cause to each mood. Example: On your commute to work, you were in a terrible mood because the traffic was jammed (or the subways were late) and you were going to be late for a meeting. You were delighted this afternoon when your boss loved your presentation, but were mighty angry this evening when your spouse forgot to take out the garbage.

Your list demonstrates that, like having a living, beating heart, being alive means there are peaks and valleys; times when we feel great, and times when we are disappointed.

A day in which you experience only one mood is a cause for concern. A day in which you experience many moods is normal and can even be the doorway to wisdom and depth.

Part III — The Anatomy of Moods

What makes a bad one bad? What makes a good one good?

Behold, man has become like one of us,
having the ability to know good and evil.
—Genesis 3:22

People are governed more by their feelings
than by reason.
—Samuel Adams

The Tripod of Your Life

Generally speaking, your life stands on three legs. When all three legs are healthy, secure, and balanced, the resulting mood is a revelation of goodness and happiness. When one or more of the legs are weak, insecure, or imbalanced, in all likelihood the resulting mood will be bad and negative.

The three legs are:
1. Who you are
2. What you do
3. What you hope for

Leg 1: Who You Are

Who you are is everything you are born with: your personality, gender, race, culture, religion, natural tendencies, social circles, family, life circumstances, inheritance, financial resources; whether you are introverted or extroverted, loud or quiet, emotional or more cerebral, calculated or more spontaneous. It usually takes a lifetime to discover every nuance of who you are, but all of us are privy to various elements that comprise who we are. For instance, you know who your parents are, how old you are, where you live, your gender, and what you believe in. All of these elements make up the first leg of life: who you are.

Leg 2: What You Do

Every human being does things. We differ in what we do, but "doing" is something we all do. Your work is something you do. Raising a family is what you "do," as is going on a diet, watching a movie, or listening to music. Do you meditate, pray, read books, or dance? Do you go to the ballet, shopping, or to the theater? Do you travel, volunteer, give charity, cook, paint, write, or sing? You do many things, and though it may be difficult to define them all, they comprise the second leg of your life: what you do.

Leg 3: What You Hope For

Your hopes and aspirations are your goals and objectives; not where you are today but where you aim to be in the future. Everybody dreams. If one has no dreams—no hopes, aspirations, goals, or objectives—then one has much bigger issues than a bad mood. An aspiration could be to get married, have children, own a home, start a business, or become the CEO of the company you are in now. A dream could be to have children, go back to school for your master's degree, or visit every continent. Whatever you strive for in the future, whatever you wish, and whatever you aspire to is the third leg of your life: what you hope for.

The more aligned these three legs are—who you are, what you do, and what you hope for—the more likely your moods will be positive. The more misaligned these three legs are, the greater the chance of having bad moods.

This next step goes a very long way to transform bad moods into good.

Defining Your Tripod: MeXercise

Take a paper and divide it into three columns. Column 1 is who you are. Column 2 is what you do. Column 3 reflects your aspirations. In each column write as many items as you can. This will not be definitive or complete; simply begin and write as many as you can.

Here is what a sample table may look like:

Sample Table (or download a printable pdf)

WHO I AM	WHAT I DO	WHAT I HOPE FOR
Age: 31	Work: Junior sales representative at a cosmetics company	Personally: fall in love, get married, have kids, grandkids
Gender: Female	Volunteer: Before holidays, I gift wrap toys for the local children's hospital / I visit retirement homes.	Professionally: want to start my own cosmetics boutique company
Nationality: American	Hobbies: love cooking, reading, skiing, playing board games, spending time with friends	Globally: want to stop hunger, achieve world peace.
Culture: Suburban middle-class	Spiritual: I meditate once a week	To write a book, learn to paint
Religion: agnostic	Entertainment: movies, concerts, travel	Misc.: Want to begin working out, eating healthfully, finding more spirituality
Personality: outgoing, funny, smart	Health: jog, go to gym	Misc.:
Family: I am a daughter and a sister	Misc.:	Misc.:

WHO I AM	WHAT I DO	WHAT I HOPE FOR
Age:	Work:	Personally:
Gender:	Volunteer:	Professionally:
Nationality:	Hobbies:	Globally:
Culture:	Spiritual:	Misc.:
Religion:	Entertainment:	Misc.:
Personality:	Health	Misc.:
Family:	Misc.:	Misc.:

Fill in the table above. As you articulate the tripod of your life, the three legs upon which your being stands, your strong points will begin to crystallize, as will your weaker points, and you will begin to see that some legs are stronger than others.

Now you can begin to see that a good mood results when who you are, what you do, and what you hope for are aligned, and a bad mood happens when they are not.

Bad Moods Are Misalignments

If a tripod has one leg that is weak, wobbly, too long, or too short, the entire tripod will be off balance. Bad moods are caused by an imbalance, when one or more of the three legs (and what they represent) are weak or wobbly. Other misalignments are when one or more of these legs is diametrically opposed to one or more of the *other* legs; when who you are is in contrast with what you do; and when what you hope for is out of sync with who you are. Look at your chart, and try to see how much of who you are meshes with what you do and what you hope for.

Bad moods aren't entities unto themselves. They do not suddenly appear from nothing, nor do they exist in a vacuum. They were, and—until you transcend them—are the result of, and reaction to, something else.

A bad mood is the result of an imbalance, be it between body and soul, potential and realization, hopes and disappointments, dreams and reality, work and family, husband and wife, or finding meaning and paying bills. It can be the clash of being where you are and where you would rather be, or any number of things. Because your bad mood is caused by misalignment and dissonance, that misalignment could be healed or realigned by achieving alignment and harmony.

The misalignment could be a bad day at work, an argument with a loved one, or pressing financial difficulties. Whatever the cause, the effect is unwelcome. It clashes with who you are, and then results in a bad mood.

Personal Example

You are a 38-year-old single woman who lives alone, doesn't date, and doesn't even go out much, yet desires to fall in love and build a family. This reflects a major misalignment between who you are, what you do, and what you hope for. You are a single woman who wishes to fall in love and build a family, yet what you *do* does not complete the picture.

Professional Example

You are a 38-year-old woman working as a junior sales associate in a corporate setting, selling cosmetics. Your dream—your long-term goal—is to run your own cosmetics boutique. One day, you get called into your boss's office. Your boss, not a terrible person, tells you that the company is downsizing and, in one month, you must clear out your desk and look for a new job.

Or you could be a 41-year-old product manager at an online company, who is expecting, finally to be promoted to a senior position. Instead, Human Resources informs you that in a month the company is outsourcing all of its tech to an outside company. But, hey, it's been nice knowing you.

You are devastated. Who you are, what you do, and what you aspire to be are suddenly misaligned. How will you ever open your own boutique without this job experience, not to mention the much-needed salary? What will you do?

Your bad mood is a direct result of this sudden disruption in your plans. In one swoop, you have lost your income, your job, and the opportunity to gain much-needed job experience.

Both of these scenarios portray a misalignment between who the person is, what the person does, and what the person hopes for. Regardless of where the misalignment begins, the end result will generally be an unstable tripod. Ultimately, through the language of bad moods, the soul calls out to you to tell you that there is an imbalance here and something is wrong.

The Result: Misalignment Is Not You

The result of this imbalance is a bad mood. A bad mood turns you into a different person. The circumstances that caused the mood do not allow you to be who you normally are. The Talmudic sages of Babylonia put it this way: "When angry, the wise lose their wisdom, and the visionaries lose their vision."[4]

When you are in a bad mood, the clearheaded decisions you usually make suddenly seem to be cloudy. Shackled in that bad mood, the kind and caring person you normally are has seemingly been replaced by a grumpy and sometimes malevolent ogre. The misalignment disconnects you from your core being and conceals it in ugly darkness.

Because a bad mood changes you into a different person for a while, you could mistakenly feel that this is you, the result of your bad mood and nothing else. This is a devastating feeling. In addition to making you feel bad about

---

[4] Talmud, Pesachim 66b.

yourself, it makes you feel hopeless, turning you into a victim of circumstance instead of a victor conquering a difficult situation. The bad mood's negative influence over you turns you into the controlled and not the controller, the servant and not the king.

It is therefore imperative—unequivocally essential—that you realize that a bad mood is a result of a misalignment and not who you are in your core being. Your bad mood, caused by a part of you that is shaky, is your soul telling you that something is off and you must find the part of you that is deeper than this. **A bad mood is an opportunity for you to discover and remember who you** *truly* **are**—existing prior to the bad mood's onset and existing after the bad mood fades—so that you may use your core self to dissolve and vaporize the bad mood that is *not* who you are.

Based on this premise, your mission, then, is to realign that which has been misaligned. If your core essence is alignment and balance, and for whatever reason something happened that caused a misalignment and imbalance, then the right tools, perspectives, and guidance will help you return to that original aligned state.

In the rest of the MeBook, we will offer various tools and solutions to achieve this goal.

Good Moods Are Alignments

If a bad mood is the result of a misalignment, a good mood is the exact opposite: a harmonious alignment.

Good moods result from striking the perfect balance between the three legs of life's tripod: who you are, what you do, and what you hope for.

Using the above examples from your personal and professional life, we begin to garner an understanding of what a good mood looks like— its balance and harmony—and the necessary components to replicate and compose it.

Personal Example

You are a 38-year-old single woman who works in a pleasant job. In your heart, you desire to fall in love with the perfect fellow, get married, and build an amazing family together. To this end, you define exactly what you want in a relationship and you implement accordingly, dating in a healthy manner, never settling for anything less. Simultaneously, you are open to giving of yourself and prioritizing hopes and desires over your comfort zones or the fear of committing to another person. Though your dream has not yet been fulfilled, the fact that who you are and what you are doing are both geared toward fulfilling your dream, you are being proactive and, in all likelihood, you will feel upbeat and happy; not like a depressed prisoner of a bad mood.

Professional Example

Say you are a 38-year-old woman working as a junior sales associate in a corporate setting, selling cosmetics. Your aspiration, your long-term goal, is to run your own cosmetics boutique. One day, you get called into your boss's office. A nice guy, your boss, tells you that the company is looking to fill a more senior role and he thinks that you would be perfect for the job.

You are ecstatic. Who you are, what you do, and what you hope for are suddenly more aligned than ever. You are now one step closer to opening your own boutique. This senior-level position will provide you with indispensible job experience, not to mention the much-needed salary increase!

How do you feel? Amazing! Your soul sings out in a good mood. Your good mood is a direct result of sudden, or gradual, alignment of your plans: of who you are, what you do, and the fulfillment of your aspirations.

The Result: Alignment (or Realignment) Is You

If a misalignment is not who you truly are— because it conceals your core self—then an *alignment* of who you are, what you do, and what you hope for *reveals* the power of your soul and the positive feelings that accompany it.

The following MeXercise may help define the anatomy of a good mood.

> **MeXercise:** Think of a time when you were in a good mood. Perhaps it was on your birthday or a special family occasion, when you graduated high school, your wedding day, when you landed your first job, upon the birth of a child, when your children got married,

33

when you became a grandparent, the day you retired, an occasion on which you traveled, the moment you fulfilled a lifelong dream, etc. How many parts of your life did not fit into that occasion that caused your good mood? The likely answer is zero, as everything in your life seemed to align perfectly. At that moment, it was an alignment between your infinite potential and your tangible reality, between who you are, what you do, and what you hope for.

When there is dissonance between your soul and your external life—being in stressful relationships, meaninglessness at work, finding you are bogged down by student loans, etc.— sooner or later a bad mood will rear its ugly head. But when your inner core is reflected in your external self, and your external self is dedicated to expressing your core (like on a wedding day, upon the birth of a child, or when you achieve a major accomplishment in your profession) then a good mood is the natural result.

Worse Than a Bad Mood

Darkness is much worse when it has you believing that it is stronger than light; that it precedes light and will succeed light. Even in the darkest tempests of your bad mood, you must remember that you, at your core, are light. As we mentioned above, your moods are soul expressions of your core self, of your inner spark telling you that something is wrong. This means that you are, essentially, deeper than your moods and that you rule your mood; your mood does not rule you. You precede your mood and you will succeed your mood. You were here before your bad mood, and will be here long after it is gone.[5]

---

[5] *Tanya*, Ch. 12.

Part IV — Making Moods MEANINGFUL

Nine Escalator Steps to Elevate Your Mood Upward

It is better that one is slow to anger than mighty; and one who rules over the spirit is better than one who conquers a city.
—Proverbs 16:32

Just because I'm grouchy doesn't mean I'm in a bad mood.
—Anonymous

Time to Realign

Armed with the knowledge that a bad mood is the result of a misalignment in the three legs of your tripod—who you are, what you do, and what you hope for—and a good mood is attained when these three legs are aligned, or even when you work toward realigning them, we will now begin to explore the most important aspect of this process: realigning the tripod of life.

The easiest, smoothest, and healthiest way to battle a bad mood is by *not* battling it at all, but by creating good moods, abolishing the dark mood by lighting a candle; and removing the emptiness by filling it with meaningful substance.

Don't Fight, Bring Light

Imagine a light bulb spending all its time fighting and dispelling darkness. The light bulb's ability to create light would be hampered; its purpose and efficiency compromised.

You are a light bulb. Your job is much more about creating light than combating darkness. With every minute you spend fighting your bad moods, ten minutes should be spent on producing moods that are good and "light."

This is the general thrust: Don't spend your time combating bad moods; instead, realign yourself into a good mood.

This, however, is easier said than done. To do so most effectively, you need effective tools to ensure that your bad mood does not bog you down, hinder what you do, or undermine your dreams in the process of realigning and recalibrating the legs of life.

Fires are not concerned with fighting darkness; they are too busy creating light. The best way to turn a bad mood into a good mood is not to fight the bad mood but to light up one that is good; to ignite one into light.

The theory is nice, even inspiring. The question now is how to implement this theory into practice.

The following is a step-by-step process of how to go from the seemingly unimpeachable bad mood to, ultimately, the greatest of good moods.

These are the nine steps:

1. Wait
2. Anger
3. Fuel
4. Facelift
5. Power
6. Atmosphere
7. Thought
8. Speech
9. Action

Now let's flesh out each step:

1. Wait

When you are in a bad mood, the first thing you should do is … nothing. Do absolutely nothing and simply wait. When a torrential downpour suddenly breaks out, the wisest thing to do is wait inside until the storm dissipates. When you are under the influence of a bad mood, the wisest thing you can do is to wait until its hold weakens. The bad mood itself is not negative per se, but it could cause (you to do) some negative things. Waiting for your bad mood to dissipate before you act on it will mitigate that risk.

How long you wait is less important than the wait itself. Be it five, ten, twenty minutes, the wait says, "I am in control." By waiting, you control your mood; your mood does not control you.

2. Anger

King David, one of history's great warrior-poets, writes one of the gentlest verses: *Rage and do not fail; speak to your heart while on your bed and be utterly silent.*[6] King David teaches something profound: When faced by failure, negativity, and a bad mood, it is time for you to get angry—angry at your failure. It is time to rage against that which is pulling you down. Never turn your anger against anyone, only against the bad mood itself. This is not about blaming something else or distracting form the root problem; this is simply challenging the bad mood itself, making it uncomfortable instead of it making you uncomfortable. The biggest part of you that is good and healthy must quake at the small part of you that is trying to sabotage your life. After waiting, and showing the bad mood who is boss, the next step is conjuring up anger at your self-made prison.[7]

---

[6] Psalms 4:5.
[7] Babylonian Talmud, Berachot 5a.

3. Fuel

As the raging waters may be channeled to create hydroelectricity, and the howling winds may be harvested to create wind-energy, your bad mood, and the anger you feel toward it, may be channeled into fuel. Turn the anger, which is energy, into healthy fuel to empower your engine. Harvest the anger created by your bad mood to energize your ability to make light. Bad moods themselves have no redeeming factor, but they can result in and cause great results. The proverb says, "In all toil there will be gain."[8] The third step is to use the bad mood as fuel for the good.

Use the fuel of the bad mood—the tension, the angst, the desperation—to light a fire. You have nothing to lose, so why not try to win?

4. Facelift

As mentioned, a bad mood turns you into a different person: it changes who you naturally are. Quoting previously the timeless Talmudic sages of Babylonia: "When angry, the wise lose their wisdom, and the visionaries lose their vision."[9]

Step four is remembering who you truly are. Remembering that you are an essential part of the greater human condition. Remembering that your birth is proof positive that you are special, that you matter, and that you have something unique to give to this world. You must know that the world and its Creator cherishes you like an only child.[10] Because your bad mood makes you feel bad about yourself, you will counter it by feeling good about yourself.

---

[8] Proverbs 14:23.
[9] Talmud, Pesachim 66b.
[10] *Igrot Kodesh*, vol. 4, #955.

Remember, a bad mood is your soul calling out to tell you that something is wrong. This should not debilitate you; this should remind you of your soul. Built into your DNA is an uplifted face, an uplifted disposition that can, and will, accomplish great things.[11]

5. Power

Even one tiny candle of light abolishes a vast cellar of darkness. A vast cellar of darkness can never abolish even one tiny candle of light. Light is power. Darkness is the lack thereof.

Darkness is much worse when it has you believing that it is stronger than light. Darkness is only depressing when you have the erroneous belief that you are like the darkness that comes before the light and you are like the darkness that returns after the light.

Even in the darkest tempests of your bad mood, you must remember that you, at your core, are light. You rule your mood; your mood does not rule you. Precede your bad mood with light and you will succeed your mood with light. You were here before your bad mood, and will be here long after it is gone. Begin convincing yourself and reminding yourself of your immense power, of your ability to turn anything bad into everything good.[12]

6. Atmosphere

One of the most difficult challenges is bridging the oft-seismic gap between mind and heart, between thinking and feeling. How do you develop an emotional feeling from an intellectual concept? You can very well understand that your bad mood is not you, and it is but a means to solve a problem and reach a greater place, but you nevertheless still feel miserable. It is

---

[11] Ibid., #886.
[12] *Tanya*, Ch. 12.

quite difficult to make a belief and understanding of good manifest as a good feeling.

This difficulty, however, is made easier by a healthy and inspirational environment, by surrounding yourself with positive influences, by immersing yourself in a nurturing and uplifting atmosphere, and by controlling that which you can control. Perhaps it is difficult to master and control your emotions and feelings. But, by mastering and controlling your atmosphere and environment, which you can certainly do, it will ultimately lead to mastering and controlling your temperament as well.[13]

7. Thought

You control your thoughts. At any given time, you can think whatever you'd like. You can sit in your office and think of the beach just as you can sit on the beach and think of your office.

To the mystics, this superhuman power—although it is really human, because everyone has the ability to reach this state—is called, in Hebrew, *moach shalit al halev*, which loosely translates as, "the mind rules the heart." When you are in a bad mood, think a good thought. Think of a wedding you attended, a great party, the day your child was born, that perfect date when you knew he/she was the one, the last day of school, a great family trip.

And you can make something up by dreaming about meeting the perfect person or thinking about buying your first home. Any good thought you create in your mind will bring good feelings to your heart.

8. Speech

---

[13] *Igrot Kodesh*, vol. 4, #955; *Likutei Sichot*, vol. 14, p. 256.

Similar to how you control your thoughts, you can also control your speech. You can say whatever you like whenever you like. When in a bad mood, say something nice. Find an elderly lady on the street and tell her how lovely she looks today. Call up your parents and tell them how much they mean to you. Tell your children that they can accomplish anything they like. Tell your spouse how much you love him/her. Say good morning (or night) to at least five people you would normally not say anything to. By adding this light, you will find that your bad mood is magically submerging into a mood strikingly resembling one that is good.

9. Action

Though it is harder at times, in addition to controlling your thoughts and speech, you can also control your actions. When a bad moods hits and you implement some or all of the above steps, then you can use action steps as well, to make headway into something glowingly possible.

For instance: doing something completely different, the polar opposite of what you are doing now. If you are now moping, do a dance. If you are now crying, smile. If you are now counting how much money you have, take a dollar and give it to charity.

Another example of these action steps is learning something new, be it online, in a book, or from a teacher. Whatever it is, learn something new and immerse yourself in positive actions.

This Results in Results

The result of these nine steps is the alignment of the three legs of who you are, what you do, and what you hope for. Results may vary. But unlike a drug, for example, this is not a warning but a blessing. The result of these nine steps will vary, depending on how you feel and how you act.

Let us now apply these nine steps to realign the misalignment example offered in Part III, showing how we can turn a bad mood into one that is good:

The example given there was the following:

You are a 31-year-old woman working as a junior sales associate in a corporate setting, selling cosmetics. Your dream—your long-term goal—is to run your own cosmetics boutique. One day, you get called into your boss's office. Your boss, not a terrible person, tells you that the company is downsizing and, in one month, you must clear out your desk and look for a new job.

You are devastated. Who you are, what you do, and what you aspire to are suddenly misaligned. How will you ever open your own boutique without this job experience, not to mention the much-needed salary? What will you do?

Applying the nine steps:

Wait: You will do nothing but wait until the brunt of the storm settles. Simply waiting is the first step to changing your bad mood into one that is good.

Anger: Now get angry at your bad mood and the situation that caused it: Why should getting fired bring me down? What right does losing a job have to depress me? Work yourself up into a tizzy at this intrusive shadow. Get angry—at no one and at nothing *but* your bad mood.

Fuel: Using your anger, you can turn this bad situation into fuel. Perhaps you will use this fuel to energize the engine of your lifelong dream and start building that boutique you always wanted. Perhaps you can use your anger as fuel to really understand your soul's mission and life's calling? Perhaps this fuel will drive you to find a better, more fulfilling vocation.

Facelift: You will now give yourself a facelift, lifting up your face and recognizing who you are: a son or daughter of the world. You will tell yourself that your bad mood is like a pimple on the pinky of a great humanitarian, for example. You will remind yourself that you are a compassionate human being and your infrequent bad moods are inconsequential in the face of your greater inner beauty. Okay, you got fired, but you are still you. Revel in it.

Power: All this will remind you of your power: you are light and a source of light. Period. This is a power that no job, or lack thereof, could ever squelch. As a matter of fact, now that you are no longer distracted by your job, you can unleash your light to illuminate things you couldn't do before.

Atmosphere: Because all of the previous steps exist primarily within yourself, and it is often quite difficult—maybe the most difficult—to convert the intellectual thoughts of your mind into the emotional feelings of your heart, and it is quite challenging to manifest abstract beliefs or ideas as concrete moods and feelings, you require a healthy environment and positive atmosphere to help you convert everything you know and believe into reality. This includes the people closest to you, your sphere, family, friends, and the truths you have been nurtured with. Reach out to someone close to you, such as your spouse, your friend, a mentor, or a parent. Surround yourself with your child(ren). And have these lights in your life help you feel what your mind knows: that your intrinsic DNA, your soul, is bigger and stronger than any loss of a job or bad mood.

Thought: Think a good thought. Yes, you lost your job, but think about what goodness and good things you can build with the time that is now on your hands. Think about what it would be like to have your own company, how you can make customers happy—how you can achieve your dreams.

Speech: Call up a friend, a potential business partner perhaps, and articulate to them your vision for your dream boutique. Tell someone you deeply care about how much you love them.

Action: Take some action, no matter how small, to fulfill your dream. Perhaps write down the dream name of your dream boutique and then take the action of purchasing the domain name for the website. Perhaps create a spreadsheet of the items and products you will begin manufacturing and marketing. Consider, perhaps, the target audience of your new company. Or perhaps apply to another job to gain more experience prior to going out on your own. Any action, as long as it brings you closer to aligning the three foundational legs of your tripod—who you are, what you do, what you hope for—is a good and positive action that will lead to...

Results: The result is the transformation of a bad mood into a good mood. If you implement these steps, there is no logical way that your bad mood won't begin to fade into something good. Certainly, it can't hurt to try it. You have nothing to lose and everything to gain.

Part V — Exercise (at) Your Will

Seven Meaningful Mood Exercises (MeXercises)

They shall renew their vigor, they shall raise wings as eagles; they shall run and not become weary, they shall walk and not tire.
—Isaiah 40:31

Many exercise forms—aerobic, yoga, weights, walking, and more—have been shown to benefit mood.
—Andrew Weil

Let's Get Practical

It's one thing to philosophize about changing a very important aspect in your life; but quite another to achieve that goal.

In the past chapters, we spoke mainly about changing a bad mood into a good mood but not about the actual mechanics of how to do that.

The goal of this fifth and final chapter is to present practical, relevant, down-to-earth exercises that can turn your bad moods into good moods. Based on and informed by the ideas presented above, here we will provide actionable tools. In addition to *wanting* to change, these tools will help you actually be able to *do —at will*.

If you compare this process to physical fitness, for example, you can easily understand the importance of becoming healthy and getting into shape. But it is much more difficult to actually exercise and change one's diet. Even if you had the world's best personal trainers and the fanciest exercise machines, the only way for you to effect change is to actually, and physically, eat right and work out.

Here are seven exercises, mental "fitness machines," to help you make that leap from bad moods to good! We hope you will use them early and often, and bring the light of good moods into your life whenever you will them to do so.

MeXercise #1: Adjective Reasoning

List ten adjectives to describe your bad mood (dark, hopeless, angry, empty, etc). Find the positive antonym for each one of the ten negative adjectives (dark/light, hopeless/hopeful, angry/delighted, empty/fulfilled). One helpful method to overcome bad moods is to describe on paper, using highly descriptive language (i.e., as many adjectives as possible) how negative adjectives affect you. Then, on another paper, using highly descriptive language, describe and construct an experience that will do the opposite, the antonym, to you.

If your job is putting you in a bad mood, described with adjectives such as "unhappy," "hopeless," "depressed," and "bitter," then your marching orders are to find a job that will result in the opposite adjectives, replacing "unhappy" with "joy," "hopelessness" with "hope," feeling "depressed" with feeling "liberated," and a "bitter" disposition with one of "optimism." This exercise establishes a baseline by which to set your goals. Though it isn't easy, hard work and discipline are usually all that's needed to produce results, to enhance the job you're at or find a better one. By endeavoring to find the right adjectives proactively, making them your top priority through behavior and actions, your spirits will be lifted and so will your mood.

MeXercise #2: Skill Set—As Good As Gold

Look deeply inside yourself and find your three greatest skills. They may be compassion, cooking, numbers, languages, singing, teaching, painting, etc. Write down what you believe to be your three greatest skills. When you write the words down, it helps make them concrete. How many of these three skills are you using, and how thoroughly are you using them?

Imagine that each one of these skills is a bucket full of liquid gold. Each bucket has a small hole on the bottom of it. Throughout the day, the liquid gold seeps out slowly. By the end of the day, the gold bucket is empty. If you don't use that specific skill during the day, your unique skill on that particular day is wasted and can never be reclaimed. Like the liquid gold seeping out of the bucket, though every day the bucket is replenished, only by using it can you hold onto the gold.

Every single day, every single morning your skill bucket of liquid gold is replenished. If you don't use it that day, it seeps out, creating a depressingly bad mood, from knowing that you just wasted an inimitable skill. The hopeful antidote is quite simple: Use that skill, all three skills, every day as much as possible. The result would be liquid gold. And a good, even *golden* mood.

MeXercise #3: Mood Makers—Interior and Exterior Design

In addition to your human moods, created by your emotions and feelings, there are environmental moods—moods that are created by spaces and experiences. For example, fine-dining restaurants go to great lengths to create a mood, an atmosphere that will provide its patrons with a quality experience. High-end retail shops do the same, with their floor plans, lighting schemes, window displays, and mannequin setups.

Put another way: there are internal moods and external moods. The internal moods are the ones you feel and experience. The external moods are those created with space, interior design, and architecture.

Why not design an external space to change your internal mood?

Create and host events that put others into a good mood, which will inevitably put you into a good mood. Put your mind and heart and soul into every detail of the event or experience, from the tablecloths to the room, the furniture to the candles, the food to the drink, the people to the invitations, the conversation to the seating plan, etc. These could play out as meaningful dinner parties where something soulful and meaningful is shared. Or organize meaningful book clubs where a heartfelt book is discussed, over wine, cheese, or snacks. Or perhaps arrange a meaningful film night, where you host a showing of a fascinating movie and discuss it. You could also begin a meaningful class on a sincere and far-reaching topic; or maybe a meaningful picnic outdoors, where people let down their guard and socialize; or a meaningful joke night: invite family and friends, and each person has to share at least one joke with a deeper insight.

The ways of creating atmosphere are many. The result will surely be a personal good mood for you, not to mention everyone involved.

The advantage of this exercise is twofold: 1) while expending energy and focusing on creating a positive experience, with all the details it entails, you will have less (or no) energy left to expend on feeding your bad mood; 2) the positive mood and atmosphere you create for the room will put you in a good mood personally.

MeXercise #4: Deep Pockets

Life is a river that never stops flowing. If you go with the flow, your bad mood will flow along with you and, the longer it remains with you, the more its negativity will increase. Because life and time flow unceasingly, it is essential to have designated times and spaces that transcend the river of time and the flow of life.

Let's call these dedicated times and spaces "pockets": pockets of time and pockets of space that remain pure no matter how fast the river rages, or to where.

Designate pockets, a pre-designated and predefined time in your day that you will never allow to be affected or infected by your bad mood. Create a pure pocket before going to bed every night, never allowing yourself to go to sleep in a bad mood. Create a pure pocket as soon as you wake up by being thankful for this day, never allowing yourself to start the day in a bad mood. Other pure pocket ideas may be designated times throughout the day for prayer—perhaps in the morning, in the afternoon, and in the evening—when you stop to reflect on something higher than the unrelenting river flow of life. Prayer does not have to be a religious experience; it just has to be real.

Creating pure pockets that transcend the normal flow of life—sacred spaces into which bad moods are uninvited and unwelcome—will demonstrate that you are in control. They allow breathing room for you to stop any negative cycle.

MeXercise #5: MeDitation

As mentioned, bad moods are myopic, focusing only on the tiny picture of troubles that are here and now. This "exercise machine" will help you work out the muscle that allows you to see the bigger picture, freeing you from the bad mood's narrow-minded trap.

Log on to your computer or smart device. Open a map application: Google Maps, Apple Maps, or another. Type in your current location and bring it up in the map. Zoom into your current location as much as possible. The more you zoom into a specific current location, the less you see of the bigger picture. A bad mood is like zooming in so close that you cannot see the rest of the world, even the people around you, which may cause you to hurt the people around you.

Now zoom out, as much as possible. The further back you zoom, the less significant your current location becomes, the less important your bad mood becomes. If you zoom back far enough, the bad mood disappears completely.

When in a bad mood, zoom out for a second and achieve perspective.

MeXercise #6: Candle Light

Buy a candle and place it on the table in front of you. Look at the candle and write down every detail you see. Write down the wick, the wax, the color, and the shape.

Now, light the candle. As you watch the flame flicker and dance, write down everything you see. The lit wick, the melting wax, the changing colors and shape, the light and heat from the flame.

Now, turn off the lights in the room.

Sometimes it takes a dark mood to remind you of your bright flame. This exercise compares your bad mood to a dark room. If you don't have a candle, the dark room of your bad mood is devastating. But because you *are* a candle—*The candle of the Divine is the soul of man*[14]—the dark room of your mood becomes the means by which you begin to see and appreciate your inner light.

MeXercise #7: Smiley Face

Smile—quite literally. Stop reading, look up (both literally and figuratively) and smile. Now smile again. You are alive. Smile. You are beautiful. Smile. You have so much to give to this world. Smile. You are indispensable. Smile. You can achieve what no one ever before, no one now, and no one in the future can achieve. Smile!

Every time you smile, your lips part and you open yourself up to greater possibilities. Though the scientific literature on smiling is relatively nascent, there is evidence that smiling can change your mood for the better, and may even be a positive contagion.[15] When you open your mouth to smile, you also open your mind to smile, and your heart to smile, and your soul to smile. A smile on your face is a reflection of the smile in your inner being. Smile then, early and often.

---

[14] Proverbs 20:27.

[15] https://www.psychologytoday.com/blog/cutting-edge-leadership/201206/there-s-magic-in-your-smile.

Postscript — Sum of the Parts

All goes according to the conclusion.
—Talmud, Berachot 12a

We shall not cease from exploration, and the end of all
our exploring will be to arrive where we started and know
the place for the first time.
—T. S. Eliot

In this MeBook, *Toward a Meaningful Mood,* we began by discussing our search for bad mood solutions, defining our bad moods and learning the steps to overcome them.

We then explored three questions that can help us analyze the cause of our bad moods:
"Why do I have moods?"
"Where do my moods come from?" and
"What would my life look like without moods?"
We spoke about objective data (something that's true for everyone) and subjective moods (the personal way you relate to and react to objective data) and the revelation that moods are a human gift.

In the third chapter, we discussed the "tripod" of your life—the three "legs" of the tripod:

1. who you are;
2. what you do; and
3. what you hope for in life.

We explored the tripods of various people and how their bad moods resulted from an imbalance between these three, showing an example that we can emulate.

In the fourth chapter, we discussed our need to realign the three legs of our "tripod." We discussed the nine steps that can be utilized to swing from a bad mood into the greatest of moods, which are:

1. Wait
2. Anger
3. Fuel
4. Facelift
5. Power
6. Atmosphere
7. Thought
8. Speech
9. Action

In the fifth chapter, we got practical, providing seven real-life exercises to help turn your bad moods into good.

Goodbye Bad Mood. Hello Good Mood.

You may have begun reading this MeBook with a dark disposition and a bad mood. As you flipped through its digital pages, you remembered that you are, essentially, a powerhouse. This might as well be your motto:

> I am a divine soul bursting with infinite potential, whose illumination the world thirsts for.

Because your inherent gifts, skills, talents, and abilities are stronger than any momentary weakness and more powerful than a bad mood, you can use every dark moment as an impetus to reach deeper and achieve more.

You have now discovered exercises and meditations to help motivate you to change, skills to help implement that change, and tools to realign your core being with your daily living. As you progress in life and grow constantly, the words of this MeBook remain ingrained in you, traveling with you wherever you may go. Anytime a bad mood threatens you, you simply have to access what you have read, in order to turn any bad mood into a good mood.

We hope that this MeBook has given you perspective and tools: to transform a bad mood into a source of and catalyst for light; to allow a bad mood to teach you something meaningful about yourself and the world; and, ultimately, to place yourself in a wonderful and positive place where bad moods can become a thing of the past.

As with all journeys, destinations are reached step by step. Though at times the road may seem winding and rough, as long as we are moving forward, and doing so together with those we care for and love, any obstacle or challenge becomes an impetus for greater growth.

It has truly been a wonderful, meaningful, and elevating journey. The greatest joy for us at The Meaningful Life Center is to know that you have found some practical guidance in these (electronic) pages, that these words will stay with you and you with them, and that the next time a bad mood comes knocking on your door, you can draw upon the resources presented here.

Please look out for more MeBooks as they begin populating the digital universe. And please contact us with any thoughts, feelings, suggestions, or anything else you may wish to share with us. There is nothing we enjoy more than hearing from you.

Thank you, and may you go from meaning to meaning, and from strength to strength, onward and ever upward.

Until next time,

Your MeBook friends at the Meaningful Life Center

Journeying together with you through this MeBook was a true honor and privilege. The Meaningful Life Center is proud to bring you tools and skills for bettering the quality of your spiritual and material life. If you liked this MeBook, you will love the best-seller which has transformed many lives, Toward a Meaningful Life[16] by Rabbi Simon Jacobson.

Get your FREE supplemental download *How to Have Your Prayers Heard*[17] now.

Subscribe to our a FREE weekly newsletter[18] that transforms lives and brings the Meaningful Life Center to your inbox.

Please post your feedback and leave a positive 5-star review on Amazon.

Please suggest topics close to your heart you'd like to us cover in future MeBooks by emailing us at: wisdomreb@meaningfullife.com.

---

[16] https://www.meaningfullife.com/product/toward-meaningful-life/

[17] https://www.meaningfullife.com/howtopray

[18] https://www.meaningfullife.com/subscribe

Made in the USA
Columbia, SC
05 January 2021

30291062R00033